CASTING

CASTING

Poems by

Robert Claps

Antrim House
Bloomfield, Connecticut

Copyright © 2021 by Robert Claps

Except for short selections reprinted for purposes of
book review, all reproduction rights are reserved.
Requests for permission to replicate should
be addressed to the publisher.

Library of Congress Control Number: 2021931152

ISBN: 978-1-943826-80-3

First Edition, 2021

Printed & bound by Ingram Content Group

Book design by Rennie McQuilkin

Front cover photo courtesy of the *Meriden Record Journal*

Author photograph by Paul Baldassini

Antrim House
860.217.0023
AntrimHouseBooks@gmail.com
www.AntrimHouseBooks.com
400 Seabury Dr., #5196, Bloomfield, CT 06002

*This book is dedicated to the memory of my parents,
Frank and Josephine Claps.*

Acknowledgments

Grateful acknowledgment to the editors of the following publications in which these poems first appeared, at times in earlier versions:

Atlanta Review: "Geography Class, 1961"
Cider Press Review: "Impatiens"
Connecticut Rover Review: "Jump Shots at Sixty," "At the Four Corners Market," "Redemption," "Building the Gate"
Crab Creek Review: "Blues for Carol"
Green Mountains Review: "Chore"
Here: a Poetry Journal: "River Returning," "Vernal Equinox"
Hollins Critic: "Milkweed"
Image: "Flood Light"
The Louisville Review: "Snapper"
Margie, An American Journal of Poetry: "Sign of the Cross"
The Paterson Literary Review: "Afterlife Consignment"
Poet Lore: "My Geese," "The Drivers," "Horseshoe Crabs Mating"
Saint Katherine Review: "Nature Poem with Recyclables"
South Dakota Review: "Map Making, 5th Grade," "Climbing the Hill Pasture"
Tar River Poetry: "Casting," "Shot Putting," "The Winter Dance, "In Cursive," "In Cursive II," "Clam Digging in Connecticut," Card Game at the Italian Club," "Learning the Planets"
Two Bridges: "Nothing but Net," "Pickerel"
The Willlimantic Chronicle: "Clam Digging in Connecticut"

"Jump Shots at Sixty" was nominated for a Pushcart Prize by the editors of the CT River Review and won its 2018 poetry contest.
"Geography Class" was reprinted in the *Atlanta Review's* 10th Anniversary issue.
"Card Game At the Italian Club" also appeared in an edition of the *Anthology of Magazine Verse and Yearbook of American Poetry*

I am grateful for my family and friends, who have shaped my life and helped make this book possible. Thanks in particular to my wife Carol, whose faith and strength have inspired many of these poems. Also a big thanks to Rennie McQuilkin, my editor at Antrim House, for his encouragement and for bringing this book to fruition. Thanks in addition to Daniel Donhaghy, Peter Makuck, Jim Daniels, and Luke Whisnant for their readings and comments.

Table of Contents

I.

Jump Shots at Sixty / 5
Map-Making, 5th Grade / 6
Learning the Planets / 7
Geography Class, 1961 / 9
Sign of the Cross / 10
In Cursive / 11
The Winter Dance / 12
The Drivers / 14
Walnuts / 16
Milkweed / 17
Chore / 18
Clamming with My Son / 19

II.

The Birds of Home Depot / 23
My Geese / 24
Clam Digging in Connecticut / 25
Pickerel / 26
Snappers / 27
Casting / 28
Horseshoe Crabs Mating / 29
Vernal Equinox / 30
River Returning / 31
To a Child Sleeping Out / 32
Nature Poem With Recyclables / 33
Redemption / 34

III.

Card Game at the Italian Club / 39
At the Four Corners Market / 40
In Cursive II / 42
Climbing the Hill Pasture / 43
Shot Putting / 44
Blues For Carol / 45
Afterlife Consignment / 46
Flood Light / 48
Building the Gate / 50
Nothing But Net / 52
Impatiens / 53

About the Author / 55
About the Book / 56

Some things
you know all your life.
They are so simple and true
they must be said without elegance, meter and rhyme,
they must be laid on the table beside the salt shaker,
the glass of water, the absence of light gathering
in the shadows of picture frames . . . .

                    from "The Simple Truth," Philip Levine

CASTING

I.

Jump Shots at Sixty

I could take a ride down Route 5 again, pull up to the rims rusting
 between the Catholic church and the train tracks,
I could ignore the fleeting back pain and dismiss my doctor's good advice
by dribbling down the length of the court, dodging the broken glass
 and chunks of asphalt,
and stopping just inside what's left of the foul line for a jump shot,
 a little mid-range one
that I will take for my father, for his wavy black hair slicked back and
 shining, and that tipsy Dean Martin weave he did at weddings,
 crooning "Send Me A Pillow To Cry On" to all the women,
and maybe a shot off the backboard for the day he took me and my
 first love to the state fair with the side money he made fixing cracked
 engine blocks,
and here, at the wing, a fade-away for his first-born infant's grave,
 and his brother's three rows down,
and a baseline shot for the blessèd plastic statue he kept on the
dashboard of his '62 Chrysler New Yorker, a miniature Jesus that
 couldn't save him from the Thorazine and dozens of electric shocks
 at the West Haven V.A.,
and how about a Dave Cowens shot, that half-hook, half-jumper, for
 the million Camels and the nips of Seagram's despite the strokes
 and the amputated toes,
and a Hail Mary for the black-and-white of him waving from a troop
 train leaving for Quantico, 1943, his eyes cast down as if looking for
 a sign, the way his eyes looked down at the waxed floor when I left
 him yesterday, gripping his walker in a room he shares with strangers,
and for that photo I keep on my desk, a final lob from three-point land,
my right elbow tucked in tight, making the ball arc so high
 I can whisper a prayer
in the moments before it falls back to earth.

Map-Making, 5th Grade

Home from the veterans hospital,
my father lingers in the kitchen
lighting another Camel while I
open our *World Book,* trace
the lower forty-eight, and then
for extra credit start on the rivers,
using the blue pencil he whittled
to the sharpest point,
making myself useful, he says,
watching me draw, first the Saint Lawrence,
then the Mississippi, which he
spells out in the voice just
strong enough to make me think
now he's all right, this ex-marine
who said little about the weeks
he spent walking the hospital's east wing,
not one word about the green pills
he kept in his top dresser drawer,
nothing about the electroshock treatments
or the nights he woke up sweating,
just this hovering close to the kitchen table,
the smell of cigarettes strong
as he bends over that map,
following with his finger the curves
of the Hudson, the Ohio,
tracing each river back to its source
where I drew them the thinnest,
blue thread stretched almost to breaking.

Learning the Planets

And childhood is distant, as distant as the rings of Saturn.
                                        Charles Wright

All morning, following the concentric circles
Sister had chalked on the schoolyard blacktop,
we walked counterclockwise, orbiting
Cindy Kowalski, the tallest in that third-grade class,
Sun written on the flash card
taped to the front of her white pleated blouse
just below the silver cross on her silver chain,

Sister shouting, "Imagine a line going through you,"
making us spin slowly around it while we walked,
Angel DeJesus, the new kid, icy dwarf Pluto,
spinning in his polished black shoes
some older kids called roach-killers,

and twenty-two light minutes away from me,
spending a second year in Sister's class
after his father took off upstate,
Eddie Cobb starting to spin out of orbit,
bumping into Jupiter, with its belts cinched tight
as Sister's woven black wool one,
worn to remind us that Christ wore chains.

The school's chain-link fence
glinted at the edge of our known universe,
and beyond it was God's kingdom,
Sister whispered, kingdom we tried to imagine,

though we could hear no trumpets
or heavenly choir, only the trucks
grinding up Center Street's hill,
while we orbited on the blacktop,
finite, and punctuated with the light
of planets following their ordained paths.

Geography Class, 1961

In my worst dreams I am back
in my seventh-grade geography class,
guessing again when Sister Teresa asked me
what Denmark's major exports are,
my knowledge of the world suspect,
though I know that Russia has the Bomb
because we drill each week,
crouching under our desks
or filing out to the concrete shelter
that fronts the armory;
and because we pray each day,
"preparing our souls for the Second Corning,"
Sister says, as she walks the aisles,
reminding us that this world will end in fire,
a sudden white flash, not the slow
burn I feel watching Kathy Simpson
clean the blackboard, especially when
she stretches, her plaid skirt rising,
her calves tightening above the brown ankle socks,
her white blouse sheer enough to show
the straps underneath,
her white arm flashing as she erases
half a continent, the pink
borders of North America gone,
nothing left but a wall of black
and the dust settling.

Sign of the Cross

A rush of cold air revived us when,
halfway through the viewing, Wendy Michaud,
the only eighth-grade girl who wore nylons,
strode through the etched-glass doors
and leaving heel prints in the carpet,
walked up to kneel at the rail where
Sister Margaret was laid out.

Mourners admiring the floral arrangements
or studying cracks in the plaster ceiling
tried not to watch her walk back down the aisle,
scenting the room with White Shoulders
while she looked for a seat;
but my eyes were on her gold glittering
lips and black-shaded eyes, the coppery
wisp of hair that kept falling across her face.

Mother Superior wrapped her rosary
tight around her fingers, waiting
for a sudden wind to make
the lilies and snapdragons tremble,
for a spirit to levitate briefly
above Sister's casket, the trumpet
of God himself to blast a warning
to the sinners among us,

But when Wendy sat next to me
and with her painted fingernail traced
the outlines of a cross on my inner thigh,
the only sound I heard was the jangle
of her bangled bracelet, and the basement
furnace switching on, a low rumbling
even the plush carpet could not contain.

In Cursive

First the bat, then the ball, Sister Agnes repeats
as she drifts down the aisles, her black robes
brushing our desks, rosary beads clacking
while we fill one page after another,
careful not to reverse a *b* or *d*, knowing
the way we write is an expression of our souls,
Sister circling my smudged erasures in red,
giving Mary Case's neat horizontal lines a gold star
and pinning them up on the bulletin board,
Mary who once asked right in the middle of catechism
if God was so merciful why wouldn't He allow
her brother to walk without braces?
Not even the winter sparrows crowding the window ledge
are able to lift our eyes from the pages
where our tall letters touch the top and bottom lines,
our *o*'s the dotted middle one, without a flourish or curl
that might show hubris,
while Sister goes from desk to desk, each one scarred
with hearts and names carved in crude block letters,
oak desks as solid as our faith should be
and anchored to the floor.

The Winter Dance

A foot-tall magnetized Jesus
gazed down from the dashboard
of my father's '62 Chrysler,
the car that reeked
of Camels, Old Spice and Schaefer's,
the car with the push-button gears,
a squared-off steering wheel,
and that broad front seat on which

we went the whole way
the night of the winter dance, my
starched white shirt and striped tie
heaped on the floor,
Carol's hard-cupped bra tossed on the dash,
swaddling His feet and the flowing plastic robes,

my eyes meeting His eyes only after we'd zipped
and hooked and buttoned up again,
when thick snowflakes began falling
under the streetlight,
some draft driving them sideways from the light
to the dark to the light again,

snow ticking against the glass
and drawing us forward to watch it melt,
the way we would melt from the heat of our sins,
as Sister Agnes had whispered,
making us hold our hands

palms up, so that she could feel
right there in the decorated gym

who was cold, who was hot,
snow coming down hard now
as we revved the engine
before the slow, treacherous ride,
and the two of us shivering
the entire way home.

The Drivers

As soon as he's out the door, my three-year-old son
climbs into his yellow plastic car
and without saying a word starts pedaling
down the steep slope of the driveway.
The last of September, and milkweed
rises and scatters in the field we face.
The leaves of the birch and the ash
and our one good maple
have begun to turn but still hold on.
I can tell by the way my son holds tight to the wheel
by the way he doesn't bother to wave
or beep the horn
that he means business, this
unswerving boy gathering speed,
ignoring me when I shout for him to brake
the way I ignored my father's *keep it under fifty*
one Sunday when I sat beside him
in the old Impala,
breathed the staleness of his Lucky Strikes
and learned how to drive.
Rusting freight cars and the twin
smoking stacks of Allied Chemical
drifted backwards in the rear-view
as we headed south toward New Haven
and its great university.
I gave it more gas
and my father's face darkened
the way it did when I spoke about books
or of wanting to write.
Keep it under fifty, he said again, his voice
louder this time, rising above the radio

and the tires' high- pitched humming,
rising again now in my throat
as I chase after my son, shouting
all down the driveway for him to *brake, brake,*
knowing that he will shoot out into the road,
that I am as powerless to stop him
as I am to stop these leaves and milkweed spores
from scattering everywhere.

Walnuts

Clear October, no songbirds left,
not one warbler or vireo,
just these grackles filling our oaks,
thousands of them, with all their radiance
cloaked in black; I'm raking the walnuts
into piles so the mower will smash
the thick, pitted husks,
and we can roast them on the grill,
salt the kernels and eat.
When I plant my foot, wind up, kick, and pitch
one deep into the woods, the rich
brown stain it leaves on my fingertips
reminds me of my mother's walnut tables,
her walnut crucifix, even the scratched antique
dresser with matching glove boxes,
which she insists I take after she is *gone* –
that hard, no-nonsense, word she prefers.
If I told her those grackles were angels of the Lord,
she wouldn't buy it, even now,
this close to death, with her voice thin as walnut stems,
not a songbird left, the nodding
branches almost bare,
and there above them,
the grackles rising in a dark river.

Milkweed

Dry October, the roadside asters gone to seed
   and beginning
to blacken, except for a few late bloomers
flaring now in the last hour of daylight;
I leave the road and trespass onto our neighbor's field
where the milkweed stand on thin stems
and do not waiver when I snap one,
bringing to my lips the bitter milk,
when I split a ripened pod and watch its froth
   of seeds take flight.

Like thousands of miniature angels' wings, the seeds,
I imagine, might ferry my mother to something
   like paradise.
How many more falls will she witness,
her heart grown fragile as dried milkweed pods,
her voice thinning like the woods backing this field,
where the black limbs have broken out
   and become a framework
for October's quick dark

Chore

Not this fungus ignored
all summer, swelling
between joist and subfloor,
but an overwhelming wish to be useful,
gets me kneeling in November's
small allowance of light,
laying out sandpaper, sealant,
and putty knife.
Facing north, on the verge
of being sold, the house trembles:
tonight, with its drapery taken down,
each room seems larger,
and mother has what she wished for
on cleaning days
when she cursed tight corners.
Now, rot flakes under the first showing
of winter stars, the bright edge
of weather we believe
we've been preserved against.
Sanding the joist clean as November light,
as white clapboard,
I begin to learn how wood works:
shrinking or holding moisture
until your home no longer fits.

Clamming with My Son

Again this summer you and I
hook into waders and stagger
thru tidal mud until

we find our balance
and follow the channel
out to the salt pond

where you, at twenty, bring up
quahogs, empty mussel shells,
muck, even a spider crab

bristling in the tines of the rake
we've inherited, the two of us
drifting toward the causeway,

past cormorants, mythic birds
believed to carry messages
from the dead, grooming now,

one to a piling, their plumage
brightly iridescent
on this day so filled

with my parents' presence
I could leave here
and ride the elevator again

up to the ICU's of their last days,
dampen their foreheads
and cracked lips with a wet cloth,

hear my father refusing
Last Rites, or my mother
calling for her long-dead sister

and yet still be here with you,
as our rakes scratch up stone
or shell until we've caught our limit

in these few hours you'll forget,
probably, before long,
our wire buckets brimming,
cutting with their weight,
leaving their impermanent marks.

II.

The Birds of Home Depot

Those sliding glass doors open automatically
and l lead us into the garden,
haloed with birds, their hundreds of ordinary
wings already starting to lift us:

dun-colored, common finches and sparrows,
maybe a pair of mourning doves, all
homesteading in the metal rafters above
the garden department. Not a songbird

among them, yet their nattering comforts us
as we compare prices on motion-sensor
lights that promise to secure our borders.
We can forget, briefly, the Rams and F150s

idling outside, with their smiling skull decals
or *Black Rifles Matter* bumper stickers.

My Geese

That moment at dusk when the flock
moving east to west broke into view
and advanced in loose formation over the paved
acres of Wal-Mart,
I knew they were my geese, not Galway Kinnell's
following the Connecticut River,
or Carruth's sounding in the night over Syracuse.
Music blasting from a parked Toyota
erased there – what was it – discourse, prayer?
No one in that lot was filled with longing.
Stopped besides my shopping cart, I watched them,
ordinary geese that perhaps had squandered the day
and now were hauling unheard
past Midas Muffler and Mister Donut,
trying to redeem themselves before dark.

Clam Digging in Connecticut

These flats marine biology majors seeded a few years back
today draw out my father in his walker, steadying
himself above the wrack line, and I with long-handled rake
and wire basket wading waist-deep, watching two
industrious mute swans in the middle of the salt pond
dipping in unison for the smaller clams, their bodies resembling
the line of clouds floating overhead, backed by September's
fragile blue. Sun-struck, wearing a t-shirt with cigarettes
tucked in the sleeve, my father once flashed white here
when he filled a half bushel basket by noon, years before
muck from General Dynamics shut down the beds.
When quahogs clink in my rake's steel tines, I offer him one;
whorled, gray with purple stains, trailing strands of eelgrass,
it smells of summer. For us, each day is more unstable
than barrier dunes in hurricane season. I think about his last
x-ray, the dark shadowy mass on his lung, the bed
that cancer has seeded. Out in the bay, the bivalve creatures
burrow deeper, holding close to the bone of the planet,
from which those winged emissaries of the gods cannot pluck them.

Pickerel

Who could blame us for believing
runoff from Allied Chemical had morphed them
into fluorescent three-eyed creatures
that grew as long as Louisville Sluggers,
fattening on frogs and hatching ducks
in the pond behind the ball field,
their chainmail sides riddled with wounds
and flashing as they fought each other
over bits of hot dog we tossed in before games.

The chain link fence our fathers pressed against
during games could not contain their cursing
when one of us struck out or got brushed
back by a fastball high and inside; sometimes
they fought among themselves
over whose son should've been benched.

Each spring, for a few weeks a male pickerel
guarded the nests that ringed the pond,
then disappeared into the deeper pools,
under pads, or among reeds,
where they lucked all summer,
needled-nosed, territorial brutes,
poised to ambush even their own young.

Snapper

Late April, and the snapper that lives
in our neighbor's pond
comes clattering up the gravel drive
with legs thick as a child's wrists,
stretching its neck when I step off the porch,
a creature as old as original sin
plodding past the swing set, keeping
one eye on the cat who hunches her back,
the other on me as I guard the garage
and the pets' brimming bowls.
Even when I take a quick step toward him
he won't scare, won't retreat,
instead lifts his horned beak and hisses
a warning, his cold
unblinking stare making it clear why
Sister Theresa at our sixth-grade science fair
crossed herself, passing my reptilian exhibit,
touching her black rosary beads as she looked
away from the forked tongues,
the splayed toes and the shiny clay tails,
whispering a *Satan be gone,*
the same words I utter today
before reason takes hold,
when the turtle, who retracted
at the introduction of my stick,
clamps onto it the second time
and does not let go, wanting, I think,
to drag me back down the drive
and into the pond that has no name.

Casting

He teeters at the edge of the dock
after his fourth rum and Coke, and still
refuses to leave, waving us off as
the first fat drops hit us and
we call him to come inside.
Even with lightning just off to our west,
he won't stop casting into the dark,
the gold blades of his lure
flickering for a moment,
then disappearing again,
all of us knowing our friend's brain
works like that: the erratic signals,
the sudden twitches that started a few months back,
the numb leg, the simple words he'd scramble,
all of us knowing he is inoperable, giving him
six months, maybe a year,
but for now there's a splash of the gold Phoebe
and our drunk friend shouting that the big ones
strike at night,
a few of us nodding as though we understand,
while the lightning and the lure flash
in a pattern we try to make sense of, but nothing
makes sense, not the nonexistent smells he smells,
not the friends' names he cannot recall,
only this casting in slow retrieval,
and he insisting as it now starts coming down hard
that any moment now
he might hook a bass or even a rainbow.

Horseshoe Crabs Mating

At the mouth of the river two miles down
from the decommissioned nuclear power plant,
a male horseshoe has crawled
onto the back of his counterpart, and now
the two are moving in tandem
as slowly as the spring fog lifts.
Their barbed tails write themselves
in thin ridges of silt,
stitching the riverbed with the threads
that maybe connect out lives to theirs,
their shells black as an old family Bible,
speckled with green and glistening
as we inch toward them, the clambering male
and the calm female,
both taking us in, one extended eye at a time,
both holding close regardless of who we are
or of what mark our kind will leave in the mud.

Vernal Equinox

The brook out back, frozen a week ago, has unlocked,
And now the first peepers, that chorus of tiny tree frogs,
punctuate the dusk. Due east, a full moon
sits on the horizon, bright as our brass floor lamp.
The Mayans built pyramids for this moment;
druids and pagans gathered at Stonehenge;
the Saxons held a feast for their goddess of fertility;
my mother celebrated spring by scanning
the sale racks at Bloomingdale's
for something to wear at Easter Mass.

Now, in our new millennium, a pyramid of plastic trash
twice of the size of Texas floats in the Pacific,
its great tangles of ghost nets ensnaring seals.
What else can we worry about?
Our school board is upgrading the building locks
and installing metal detectors;
wood smoke drifts across the yard of the house
down the street where the town council woman
with stage four cancer
works on a playlist for her funeral.

Still, for a moment, standing out here
between the brilliance and the song,
everything we know falls away.
I won't say we're changed, but you almost feel
the first green blades breaking through the loam.
Even our ancestors' stone walls, crusted
with lichens and running in all directions at once,
cannot contain those peepers
singing wildly at the edge of the woods.

River Returning

Every evening now, a Great Blue gliding
down through the oaks just leafing out
stands motionless on these banks, where
growing up we threaded our way among
bald tires, dead carp, leaking barrels
of solvents the mills our fathers worked at
dumped when no one was looking.
Wasn't the river ours to burn?
Three shifts a day with all the overtime
you wanted turned the water green
but even Uniroyal couldn't kill it
and the river is growing young again:
spawning shad find the ancient ruined
channels and run upstream in numbers
no one living remembers. Yet the oysters
of Long Island Sound work overtime
to filter out the particles of this century's
plastic waste. How tenuous it all is.
Watch the infant oak leaves tremble
as you move quietly, hoping to get closer
before the wings creak open
and without moving the Blue is gone.

To a Child Sleeping Out

With nothing behind you but
darkening woods, you could believe
it's pterodactyls, not airplanes,
Passing overhead.

Ahead, only the duplicate homes,
lives boxed in by repetition
and the urge to possess;
so kiss us goodnight.

You won't go far
but the crickets' small talk
will seem more wild, there
at the depth of yard's edge.

Nature Poem with Recyclables

October, at the flawless end to a year of I.E.D's
and suicide bombers, the grackles arrive in great
clusters to pepper these oak crowns, nodding
on a narrow strip between the interstate and the Price
Chopper parking lot, where we in the middle
of our chores stop to listen: their shrill calls
punctuated by the contrabass of the big rigs
soaring into that unrelenting blue, morphing, I swear,
into song. Even the sullen teenager gathering
shopping carts strewn across the lot removes his
ear buds and looks heavenward. The carts can wait.
Better to learn how to stand guard against despair
than to busy ourselves otherwise, like that guy
dressed in camouflage and hauling black plastic bags
brimming with empties into the store for redemption.

Redemption

Six of us in line already this early
Saturday morning, our heads bowed as if
to better contemplate our shopping carts
and trash bags brimming with empties,
we wait for the doors of ShopRite's
redemption center to open, and why I'm
reminded of my second grade class waiting
in line for our first confession, I can't say.
No one here is holding a rosary or whispers prayers,
though one woman wired to earphones and lifting
her closed eyes upward, softly sings. And
the balding guy in greasy shorts and work boots
hiding behind his mountain of beer cans
can't recall last night much less sins
he'd want confessed.   Shop-Rite's doors
slide open promptly at eight, and maybe it's
the meekness we enter the windowless room with
that helps me recall the confessional's hard bench
and kneeling rail, the faint odor of Father Sullivan's cigars,
and that certain weightlessness we felt as we left
the church, floating down the great stone stairs,
our penance done, the burden of our second-grade
sins lifted for a while.
Maybe it's how this boy, eight or nine, feeds
the shredding machine, holding each can up
like it's his offering to the world, the baseball cap
he wears backwards barely containing his excitement
to be getting his first skateboard – "His reward,"
the father winks, "for helping with the cans."

You could tell that, already, the boy
is screaming down the Church Street hill,
elevating over the curbs, his feet
not once touching the ground.

III.

Card Game at the Italian Club

Surely it is more than past time,
the backroom booths removed
from the afternoon,
the stained fingertips stacking change,
the hands scarred from machine-shop years
waiting idle and damp for the cards'
plastic slap, the liquid coughs
welling up from the chest, then settling again.
From the bar, music drifts in, and
wing-tips tap on the oiled wooden floor.
But nothing stirs them or hurries
their pleasure; even the high idle
of homebound traffic, stalled and
steaming at the Route Five light,
can't crack Montovani's lush walls.
Day after day, deliberate and cautious,
they bid on the smallest stakes,
wanting only to break even.

At the Four Corners Market

She's here too, no make-up,
same cardigan sweater
buttoned at the neck, glasses
swaying on a silver chain
as she rings me out,
this time disguised as a clerk
working on a register behind
a neon *Lotto* flickering
in the front window of the Salem
Four Corners Market on Center Street, Salem,
small-boned graying woman who greets me
with my mother's half-smile,
who makes her birdlike motions,
that quick opening and closing of the hands
as she takes my gallon of milk,
passing it through the scanner's
beam with the same wide
circular sweep of her arms
my mother made, wiping down
the counters and the kitchen table
back on Orchard Street
after her firstborn's crib death,
after her husband's electroshocks
and years of two-packs-a-day,
using elbow grease to bring out the shine,
the petite clerk and my mother
both sad as I shake my head
at the Slim Jims and the little
fruit pies, the apple, the cherry,
the two women calling me back
as I start to leave, pointing

at the jackpot sign, whispering
the birthdates of a favorite aunt,
the street address of a first house,
numbers they promise will bring me luck.

In Cursive II

As if to show us again why she was named
the 1940 Palmer Method Penmanship
Champion of South Philadelphia High,
signing copies of her living will here

in the lawyer's office,
she flexes her wrist to make the upper-case *J*
a full inch taller and without lifting her pen
connects it to the *o,* coming back to dot
the *i* only after *Josephine* is complete,
each letter slanted and flowing so perfectly
I'm reminded of those second-grade drills
we practiced to make our letters touch
The top and bottom blue lines, page after page
piling up each night at our kitchen table,
the difficult *p's* or *q's* drawing her close,
the scent of Aqua Net stinging my nose
as we made a *B* for Baldy's Tap –

your father's second home –
or an *E* for Elsie, her first-born who rests
near my father at St. John's cemetery,
papers scattered there across our table, and here,
where the lawyer hands her one last copy
and my mother is careful to make her
letters touch the black unbroken line,
the floor on which all letters rest.

Climbing the Hill Pasture

The morning after our first hard frost,
finding in among bramble thickets
a skull – chipmunk, maybe –
and the feathery traces of a few trampled souls
makes me wonder who else
is hovering unseen beside me,
my father, gone three years, now
light as milkweed spores,
here to remind me that I still have a temper,
that too often my eyes stray,
that I don't deserve my wife and daughters,
and floating beside my father
the unborn one says nothing,
though at times a gust in the oak crowns
or a squirrel rustling the tall grass
forms a tiny infant voice
so hushed I have to stop to hear it.
One eye on the high thin clouds
coming in now from the east,
wishing now I had brought a flannel
jacket instead of this nylon one,
the sunlight fading the way
those invented voices have,
though they will return, giving me
little reprieve no matter how many
Our Fathers I whisper, studying
the ground and the overgrown hedges,
bending to touch the weeds,
sumac's darkened cones,
goldenrod gone to seed,
the asters' blackened hearts.

Shot-Putting

He'd stand at the back of the circle, eyes
focused on the oak-crowns
swaying at the edge of the field,
in the blue above them, gauging
wind direction or the nearness of God,

the twelve-pound shot cold
and cradled under his chin,
glinting as he'd lean forward and
balancing his weight on one leg, begin
his backward glide under an April sun

that shone brilliant on our blue
and white high school uniforms,
the black cinder track, the chrome
on our parents' cars parked in the lot,
even on the gold ring on my good friend's hand,

the one he drove upward,
sending with the flick of his wrist
the black steel ball high above us,
the arch of it reaching into my back deck,
where I sit, decades after his death,

hearing it thump the spring grass.

Blues for Carol

March, the month of your oldest daughter's death,
sky the grey of windfall branches scattered across
the yard, and the finches at the feeder just as drab;
two days into spring, the maps show bands of snow
inching up the coast, but down by the mailbox, defiant,
the crocus, pushing aside gravel thrown by the plow
and leaves matted inches thick, sticks out its tongue.
Can the small things of this world still comfort?
Red as your nail polish or a sanctuary lamp,
and flitting at yard's ungoverned edge,
a cardinal, that bird you take as a sign, cannot
hold its tongue, breaking out a *cheer, cheer,*
even as the storm arrives in sheets of heavy flakes
that wrap around our house.

Afterlife Consignment

My wife still talks about those floral brocade pumps,
sling backs with calfskin trim and leather lining,
"a four-hundred-dollar pair and hardly used!"

She still frequents the sale racks at *Savvy Swap,*
where, last year, she found that leopard print sweater,
not to mention the hand-made Italian

silk shirt with flared sleeves
she couldn't afford, until the owner
knocked off an extra ten per cent,

and later sent a link to her Facebook page
for grieving mothers.

Bless *Deals N' Steals,* and *Saks Thrift Avenue,*
trying to survive among the dead
mills and seedy dealerships on Route 6 –

bless their facades of pastel purple
and mustard yellow
that brighten Carol's mood

after those Sunday visits
to St. John's Cemetery.
And bless the stonecutter

for the pair of ballet shoes
chiseled perfectly into red granite,
one on each side of Carol's

oldest daughter's name,
shoes with crossed straps
and a drawstring knotted in front,

like the pair at *Afterlife Consignment,*
the ones she could not walk past
without first pausing to study

the flesh-colored canvas,
to touch the worn leather soles.

Flood Light

It's snowing, and my good friend, who
lost his youngest son a year ago,
has come to help install the new
flood light above my garage.

Our bare hands redden as we work,
he high on the ladder cutting the old
connections, and I drilling
an outlet hole through the siding.
Watching him run 14-gauge wire,

I think how steady he seems, shifting
his weight on the top rung, off meds
now for what? – a few months at least? –
his eyes clear and shining with fresh snow.

The wind wrapping around the house
is numbing, but he won't wear gloves
or come inside until he screws in
the junction box and the steel
conduit hangers.

He won't even look at me, or my wife
tapping on the window, until he's twisted
the black wires on both ends, then the whites,
taping and capping each pair,

until it's 7 P.M.
and we've been out here for hours
with the large flakes building on our shoulders,
drifting across the long gravel drive

that suddenly illuminates
when he tries the switch by the entrance,

the one at the stairs, then back
to the entrance again just to be sure,
while my wife and I
huddle on the porch to watch
his burning fingers turning the night
on, off, on, on.

Building the Gate

When I set the first picket
   on the rails,
my father, silent twenty years,
   offers his two cents, *Use your square,*
the voice coming from behind my shoulder
   and more resonant than I remember,
so deep I turn, half- expecting to see
   the perpetual Camel
dangling from his lips, flannel shirt
unbuttoned though it's barely fifty out,
   the sleeves rolled up
like he's ready for work.

What I see is our lawn, greening and lumpish
   with goldfinches,
the oaks not yet leafing out, but their trunks
groaning in the late-April wind;
   that explains the voice, you say.
Maybe you think I'm nuts or just using
   a conventional poetic device,
but it was his voice, either descending
   from the tree crowns
or arising with the first pale crocuses,
   I don't know.

I thought he was gone for good,
that practical man who dismissed
   the afterlife,
who believed only in the eight-hour
   day plus overtime,
anxious now to get busy as he ever was

those 5 AM mornings in the kitchen,
    drinking black coffee spiked
    With Seagram's.

So when he or the wind tells me
the rails and pickets aren't
    perpendicular,
I nod and reach for my square,
not wanting to piss him off,
unsure of what he will do once
the gate swings level on its hinges
    and holding it open
      I invite him inside.

Nothing But Net

Picture us, two sixty-year-olds
shooting the rock in the cul-de-sac,
me in ripped gardening jeans,
dribbling with one hand, holding
a beer with the other,
and my wife, off-balance, favoring
her good hip, ready to swear out loud
if she breaks a fingernail.
Little wonder the neighbors honk
and wave as they pass, relieved
to see us laughing again
three months after the wake,
time my wife spent out back
watching the feeder for signs
or kneeling in the garden, planting
phlox and vetch, common asters,
everything purple, except for
the three-foot angel praying
with her stone hands clasped.
I wish I could tell you
that small birds bring daily
messages from her daughter,
that the wildflowers console,
or that each shot my wife takes
forms a perfect arc and falls
through the hoop, nothing but net.
But no, sometimes she forgets
to tuck an elbow in, flick
her wrist and wave goodbye
to the ball; sometimes
she doesn't care, and when she thinks
I'm not looking she'll throw up a prayer.

Impatiens

Late May, and it's safe at last here
in Connecticut to plant impatiens,
my wife unloading flats of them, red
and white by the mailbox, pink and
three shades of purple for our front walk.
A month ago snow still covered the ground,
and Carol, the grieving mother, shut down,
letting reruns of *Law and Order*
anesthetize the afternoons. But today
even the cardinal tattooed above her heart
sings its one sweet note, peeking out
above the ripped blue tank top as she
kneels, her hands in the earth again,
this time not to feel for messages from her daughter,
but to dig holes, untangle the roots,
set in the impatiens, and firm the soil around them.

ABOUT THE AUTHOR

Robert Claps recently retired from a large Hartford, Connecticut-based insurance company, where he worked for thirty years as a software engineer. His poems have been nominated for a Pushcart Prize, and have appeared in publications including *Image, Margie: An American Journal of Poetry, Grey's Sporting Journal, Tar River Poetry, Hollins Critic,* and the *Connecticut River Review.* A father of three children, he lives in East Hampton, Connecticut where he sometimes substitutes at local schools.

This book is set in Garamond Premier Pro, which had its genesis in 1988 when type-designer Robert Slimbach visited the Plantin-Moretus Museum in Antwerp, Belgium, to study its collection of Claude Garamond's metal punches and typefaces. During the mid-fifteen hundreds, Garamond—a Parisian punch-cutter—produced a refined array of book types that combined an unprecedented degree of balance and elegance, for centuries standing as the pinnacle of beauty and practicality in type-founding. Slimbach has created an entirely new interpretation based on Garamond's designs and on compatible italics cut by Robert Granjon, Garamond's contemporary.

For more concerning the work of Robert Claps, visit
www.antrimhousebooks.com/authors.html
This book is available at all bookstores
including Amazon.

Copies of the book can also be ordered
directly from Robert Claps
at 73 Charles Mary Drive
East Hampton, CT 06424
(robertclaps@sbcglobal,net).
Send $16 per book
plus $4.00 shipping in CT
($6 shipping beyond CT)
by check payable to
Robert Claps.

www.ingramcontent.com/pod-product-compliance
Lightning Source LLC
Chambersburg PA
CBHW030138100526
44592CB00011B/938